FALKLANDS VICTORY:

Commemoration Poem

by
Kenneth John
RIDER

CENTURY HOUSE
Literature Series
Editor:
PROF. KOPAN MAHADEVA, PhD

ACKNOWLEDGEMENTS

The author has consulted numerous sources including official documents in composing this long poem, and all such information is gratefully acknowledged. In particular the works by: **Christopher Dobson et al.** (The Falklands Conflict, 1982), **Hugh and David Tinker** (A Message from the Falklands, 1982), **General John Frost** (2 Para Falklands, 1983), **Rick Jolly** (The Red and Green Life Machine, 1983), **Max Arthur** (Above All Courage,1985), **Edward Fursdon** (The Falklands Aftermath, 1988), and **Ian Strange** (The Falkland Islands and Their Natural History, 1987) have been extremely helpful in providing background knowledge.

Special thanks are due to **Max Hastings**, joint author with **Simon Jenkins** of the main source, for both material and for kindly permitting the use of maps from their book, **The Battle for the Falklands, 1982,** and **very special thanks to Major The Rev. David Cooper, AKC, for his Foreword** and friendly critical comments on the poem, and to **Susan Vile** for her frank and wonderfully perceptive critique. Finally, thanks are also due to the Author's family and friends, for all their help and understanding.

First Edition, 1993
Typeset and Published by:
CENTURY HOUSE,
99-101, Sutton Road,
Birmingham, B23 5XA, UK

RRP: £ 5.50, Postage & Packing (UK): 50p Second Class

DEDICATION

The valiant and successful British campaign to retake the Falkland Islands, seized and strongly defended by the forces of Argentina, was fought in circumstances of extraordinary difficulty and danger by the British Task Force, whose fluctuating fortunes alternately petrified and electrified the nation. The epic nature of their achievement against all the odds has seemed to cry out for commemoration in verse. This book, **Falklands Victory: Commemoration Poem,** *is an attempt, however insufficient, to supply this need. The poem is intended as a tribute to British spirit and endeavour, and is dedicated to the members of the Task Force and all others who shared in their struggle, and to the memory of those who gave their lives in striving for Britain's Falklands Victory.*

FALKLANDS VICTORY:
Commemoration Poem
by
KENNETH JOHN RIDER

CONTENTS

Foreword by Major The Rev. David Cooper, AKC,   **PAGE**
Chaplain to 2nd Battalion, The Parachute Regiment (2 Para)   5

Prologue:	*Origins of the Dispute*	6
CANTO-I:	Misjudgements : Invasion	9
CANTO-II:	Task Force : Preparation : Embarkation	13
CANTO-III:	Negotiations : The Haig Mission	17
CANTO-IV:	Naval Disasters : Plans for Landing	22
CANTO-V:	Ashore at San Carlos : Heavy Air Attacks	27
CANTO-VI:	Renewed Air Battles : Further Ship Losses	33
CANTO-VII:	Darwin and Goose Green	41
CANTO-VIII:	Advances by Land and Sea : Fitzroy Disaster	48
CANTO-IX:	The Mountain War : *Glamorgan* Damaged	55
CANTO-X:	Tumbledown: Wireless Ridge : Foes Surrender!	62
Epilogue:	*Conclusion*	67

*[The story of the Falklands War begins at Canto-I. The Prologue places the conflict in its historical setting. The Epilogue considers the immediate aftermath of the War and its longer-term consequences — **Author**]*

FOREWORD

by Major The Reverend David Cooper, AKC,
Chaplain to the 2nd Battalion, The Parachute Regiment (2 Para)

War is an all embracing activity. For the participant, it involves both the intellect and emotions. For that reason, perhaps, it is very difficult for a person who has never been at the forward edge of battle to really understand what it is like. He can engage his intellect to try to understand, but he can never feel the emotion. For the soldier who has been through that experience, no matter how eloquent he might be, he will generally fail to be able to convey to his own satisfaction the feelings and experience to one who hasn't.

It shouldn't surprise us, therefore, that so many participants in war turn to verse to try to find a more adequate means of expressing themselves. Their poetry may be good, or it may be bad, but for them its success lies in the increased satisfaction of a truer expression of their thoughts and feelings.

Along with the soldier, whose poetry is essentially a personal statement,as much for his own need as that of anyone else's, has gone the epic poet or saga writer. These too have filled an essential place in the life of a nation — at times a greater place than others, but nevertheless it has always been there.

For that reason I am delighted to have the opportunity of writing this preface to Ken Rider's work which traces the course of the Falklands War and the fortunes of those involved in it.

It does so in verse and in doing so adds a further dimension to an event in the history of our nation.

Prose alone cannot do justice to recounting an event that is all-consuming for those involved in it. When the future of our Governments also hangs on the outcome of that event then it is right that there should be a record that is more than simply a bald account of the conflict in the South Atlantic in 1982. Ken Rider has provided that account.

[Major Cooper, Weapons Expert and Bisley Marksman, was present at Goose Green and was mentioned in despatches for the leading part he played in the evacuation of casualties — Author]

5

PROLOGUE

ORIGINS OF THE DISPUTE

'Driven off course by storms we came to islands
Grass-grown with shrubs and heath, but bare of trees,
Hilly,with rocks and boulders, swept with rain,
Yet fringed with sunlit bays and graceful inlets.'
John Strong from Plymouth makes the first known landing
On islands Britain later names the Falklands.

Should man invade these rocky shores, the haven
Of seals and penguins, albatross and petrel?
None ventures here until de Bougainville,
French commodore, and Englishman John Byron
Brave southern seas to found small settlements,
Each claiming these distant islands for his sovereign.

France yields her rights to Spain, conceding her claim
They form part of her South American domain.
Spain ousts the British, who, while quitting, maintain
Their title to the Falklands still remains.
Then Spain withdraws, relinquishing these shores
To nature's own contingencies once more.

Newly formed Argentina next lays claim,
Resettles Spain's Port Solidad and names
Louis Vernet as Governor of the Islands.
Trouble flares up when Vernet rashly seizes
United States Ship **Harriet,** *for ignoring*
Seal fishing regulations. In revenge
The U.S. fleet destroys the harbourage.

6

Britain now reasserts her sovereignty,
Forces the remaining Argentines to leave
And in Port Solidad establishes
Falklands' first long-enduring settlement.

Then sheep are brought and kelpers settle here
Eking a meagre living amid these hills.
Shipments of iron and timber furnish means
To build communities. Hardware and tractors
Improve the lot of farmers. Household goods
Lighten the burden of settlers' daily toil
With wool and fish and kelp, their lasting trades.
Faster sea travel, telephones and wireless
Strengthen their bonds with home; while inland links
Are opened up by island-hopping aircraft.

Yet while the Falklands' isolation shrinks,
They still remain, as seen by Dr. Johnson —
'An island thrown aside from human use' —
Desired for the mere right of possession
More than for benefits that might accrue
To the possessor or the Falklanders.

Meanwhile, Argentina does not cease
To label Britain's seizure of the Islands
Unlawful, and to claim them as her own.

*   *   *   *   *   *   **

Appealed to for adjudication,
The Assembly of the United Nations
Instructs the British and Argentines to find
A formula to resolve their rival claims
Bearing the settlers' interests in mind.

Talks, at last, are set in motion.
Agreement is reached upon the notion
That improved communications
Must be supplied by both the nations:
Ships and an airstrip by Britain; Argentines
To operate a regular airline.
But Britain fails to carry out her bargain,
Leaving the field clear for Argentina
To reinforce her ties with the Malvinas.

Lord Shackleton, in a survey of the Falklands,
Pinpoints their future needs; but Britain's slowness
To put his plans in train shows her reluctance
To underwrite development of the Islands.
And yet a poll shows that the Falklanders
Wish Britain to remain the sovereign power.

Britain's denial of Argentina's claim
Angers the Junta, which holds her to blame
For not discharging her legal obligation —
Restoring the Islands to Argentine occupation.

[End of Prologue]

FALKLANDS VICTORY:

CANTO I

MISJUDGMENTS: INVASION

Near where the wind-soaked Falklands ride
The South Atlantic tide,
Aboard a freighter almost unespied
Sail totters — with South Georgia on their mind.
(Momentarily the state totters!)
Destination, abandoned whaling station;
Intention, demolition and reclamation.
Leith's unmanned harbour bar presents no bar
To Davidoff's gang of rash adventurers.
Unchecked, they disembark and hoist their flag.

Survey chief Martin treks from Grytviken
To order David-off. The Chief in vain
Dismisses them from Leith. Much to his shame
Martin commands no force to enforce his command.
His red card's spurned; their blue-white flag remains.

'Scrap merchants' landing' (flying sorcery?) —
The news flash stuns Port Stanley. Whitehall keeps calm,
Protests officially in Buenos Aires
And, to be safe, sends survey ship *Endurance*
To watch events at Leith.
Rumours are rife
Of romage remote in Rivadavia.
Britain's agent in Buenos Aires reports
Intense activity in Argentine ports.
Whitehall's response stays cool; merely 'sit tight'.

Her too compliant complaint makes bold the Junta.
It's high time Britain toned down her lofty tone.
Argentina will risk a scrap for her scrap merchants.
Her struggle for the islands is not flagging;
Soon will Malvinas' flag be Argentine.

A warlike mood envelops Buenos Aires:
    'How long must Argentina feel
    The imprint of a foreign heel
    On islands that, whate'er the score,
    Lie nearest to our southern shore?
    Britain's continued occupation
    Is without legal justification.
    Besides, she shows no real desire
    To longer stoke the Falklands fire.
    To-date she has not yet provided
    Improvements Lord Shackleton decided
    Essential minimum requirements
    For future life upon the islands.
    Hasn't she, in negotiations
    Proved lukewarm on her obligations?
    Britain has slimmed her far-flung navy,
    Is axeing *Endurance*, signalling plainly
    Declining interest in the region;
    A clear intention of decamping
    From islands in the South Atlantic!'

Thus Galtieri, Amaya and Lami Dozo:
With troubled Europe, an ailing economy,
Can Britain wish to retain autonomy
Of the distant Falklands? Policy suggests
She'd shed her title with suitable pretext.
Indeed in Costa Mendez's opinion
Britain seeks reasons to be rid of 'em.
A nation so beset with pressing crises
Is in no posture to defend her prizes.
With *Endurance* on watch off South Georgia
This chance to seize the islands may not reappear.
Its destination veiled in thin disguises
The Argentine fleet puts to sea for 'Exercises!'

Whitehall anxiously tries to read the star signs.
Although Argentina still lays claim to the islands
She has agreed discussions should continue.

Due to unrest over the 'disappeared ones'
The Junta badly needs some dazzling triumph
To stifle blame and boost its shaky image.
Of all exploits, regaining the Malvinas
Would win it most acclaim. Britain therefore
Should give Argentina no excuse to launch
A rash invasion we could not repel.
Supplying naval aid for her scrap merchants
Though maybe a gesture to impress the masses
Betrays a reckless eagerness for conflict
We should beware of (— a thought, alas, too late!)

Has Carrington misread the warning signals?
Did Galtieri wrong-foot the cautious F.O.?
To rectify their too-exposed position
Thatcher and Carrington quickly dispatch
Three nuclear submarines to patrol the Falklands.
Scarce done before a signal from Port Stanley,
'Argentine fleet approaching' startles Whitehall.
The news of this shattering development
Carrington glumly announces to the Lords.

A sluggish Britain is shell-shocked into action.
The Commons debate; top Ministers confer;
Complaint is laid before the United Nations;
Premier Thatcher talks long with her advisers.
Time is too short to halt the planned invasion
By force; diplomacy might still succeed.
Failing this, all endeavour must be made
To repossess the islands. In New York
A deftly worded U.N. Resolution
Bids Britain and Argentina to shun force
And solve their quarrel by diplomacy.
In one last effort to avert a conflict,
Thatcher asks Ronald Reagan via the 'hot-line'
To warn Galtieri in the plainest terms —
If Argentina's troops invade the Falklands,
Britain will use whatever force is needed
To repossess them.

With danger closing, Falklands Governor
Gutsy Rex Hunt acts out his tragic farce:
Around the islands' meagre coast defences
Deploys his force of sixty Royal Marines.
His broadcast warning of imminent invasion
Stuns the Globe Inn with utter disbelief.

Action is short-lived. Argentine commandos
Flown in by helicopter storm Port Stanley.
Thousands of troops with armour pour ashore.
Forced to engage with overwhelming numbers
The Royal Marines fight fiercely, until
Governor Hunt, seeing resistance futile,
Signals surrender.
Then as cockaded Hunt in all his splendour,
Refusing to shake the hand of victor Garcia,
Is taken like a prisoner from his islands
The blue-white Argentina flag is raised.

    *   *   *   *   *   *

Marine Lieutenant Mills, lately installed
On South Georgia to watch events at Leith,
Hearing of Stanley's fate prepares his men
For instant action. Mines are improvised
Round unprotected beaches. The Survey Team
Under Chief Martin moves inland, to safety.
To Mills' alarm an Argentine corvette
Arrives at Leith, begins unloading troops
And calls Mills to surrender. In reply
Royal Marines open fire with machine guns,
Rockets and rifles, strafing their helicopters.
The corvette, hit close to by Gustav rounds,
Moves to safe distance to bombard the British.
At this point, knowing further resistance useless
Mills offers to surrender. His tiny force
Of twenty-two Marines is first disarmed,
Then put on board an enemy patrol ship —
The Argentines astonished to discover
How small the force that put up such resistance.

[End of Canto-I]

CANTO II

TASK FORCE: PREPARATION : EMBARKATION

At length the British Cabinet resolves
Immediate action : a naval Task Force
To assemble and be manned and fitted out
And promptly sail for the South Atlantic.
But in the Commons, Ministers are blamed
For ignorance of Argentine intentions
And failure to forestall them. In vain John Nott
Protests that three weeks' notice would be needed
To circumvent an Argentine invasion.
On every side the Government's inaction
Is branded betrayal of the Falklanders.
Yet all consider Argentina's invasion
Unwarranted, and her claim to sovereignty
Without legality. Members unite
In calling for strong measures to expedite
Return of the Falklands Isles to British rule.

The Royal Navy wastes no time in acting.
Admiral Leach, First Lord, commands John Fieldhouse
To place a naval force in readiness:
Its spearhead to be the First Flotilla
Of 'Sandy' Woodward, already out at sea.
So *Hermes* and *Invincible* are loaded
With Sea Harriers for vital air support.
Type-42 destroyers armed with Sea Darts
And frigates-22 with Sea Wolf missiles
Are requisitioned for close air defence.
Ships already patrolling the Atlantic
Take on supplies at sea (risking their safety),
Then start the journey south without delay
With crews already many weeks at sea.

General Moore, commanding Royal Marines,
Recalls his staff from NATO work in Denmark
To speed the Marines' departure and to plan
Their operations in the South Atlantic.
Members of '3' and '42' Commandos
On leave, are recalled for imminent departure.
A third contingent, under Julian Thompson,
3rd Parachutes, completes the landing force.
And now the job of shipping out the Task Force
Is swiftly put in hand. Assault ship *Fearless*
Becomes Marines' command ship. *Hermes,* laden
With Sea Kings and Sea Harriers, also ships
One squadron of Commandos. Fortunately
Authority to commandeer merchant shipping
Helps Task Force planners in their choice of ships.

Their first choice, *Canberra,* the giant cruise liner,
Has room enough to ship a whole brigade
With space for vital training while at sea.
Requisitioned and brought home from Gibraltar
She's stripped right down, replenished and refurbished,
Bedecked for helicopters and equipped
For sea communications within days.
Storeships and tankers, ferries and repair ships
Are swiftly modified for naval use.
Atlantic Conveyor is chartered as supply ship.
Cruise liner *Uganda* is converted
Into a well-appointed hospital
While even *QE2,* best loved of liners
Is requisitioned for service as a troop-ship.

With equal urgency, procurement staff
Assemble vital equipment and supplies
Of food and clothing, kit and arctic gear,
Of tanks and tractors, guns and ammunition,
Of office and administration stores,
Of leisure and domestic requisites,
Goods to maintain a modern combat force
In fighting fettle. Port officials marvel
At their vast quantities, and question where
All will be stowed; but space is found in time.

But, for marines, pilots and able seamen,
Midshipmen, engineers, stokers, sea cadets,
Officers, men, commanders, naval ratings,
The signal to join the fleet's no holiday!
Ships out at sea head south without delay —
Their crews unable to say farewell to loved ones.
Others, more blest, enjoy a weekend leave
To bid farewell to family and friends,
Some ruefully postponing cherished hopes
Of weddings, house moves, plans for children's futures.
Some sadly leave behind expectant wives
To bear the pains of childbirth on their own.
Two make time race: arrange a lightning wedding,
Snatching a blissful weekend honeymoon
Before a tearful, agonising parting
At Portsmouth Harbour.

From Southsea, Portsea, Fratton and Gosport,
From Torpoint, Plymstock, Hooe and Devonport,
From round the coast and places far inland
Seamen return to man the Navy's Task Force,
Uncertain, like the nation, of the outcome
Of this endeavour, but by now resolved
To play their part in settling this dispute
Now and for good.

Embracing sadly, men and women seek
To console partners with a cheerful word,
Sad that they can't express their feelings fully —
Confused with love, with fear, with some relief
That this sad parting's not of their own making.
On Monday morning everything is ready.
Proudly the Task Force sails from Portsmouth Harbour.

Carriers *Hermes* and *Invincible*
Head the formation with assault ship *Fearless*.
Destroyers, frigates, RFA supply ships
Follow in line astern. Huge crowds of people
Cheer and wave flags and wish them safe return.

And wives and girl friends (some of brief acquaintance)
Weep as they see their beloved sailor boys
Lining the decks of ships bound for the sea.
The moment passes; sirens, hooters, bands
Make thought impossible. As they gather way
And move into the distance, on the air
From many amplifiers come these words:

> *"God bless you, dear sailor; keep you from all harm.*
> *My love will enfold you till you're in my arms.*
> *Come back soon, dear sailor; but while we're apart,*
> *My love, I will hold you right here in my heart."*

Slow down the Solent the new armada sails,
Beyond Biscay and so into the Atlantic
To join with the contingent from Gibraltar:
Destroyers *Glasgow, Coventry* and *Sheffield,*
Exeter and *Cardiff;* and doughty frigates
Broadsword, Brilliant, Ardent and *Avenger;*
And so the Task Force sets about its task.

[End of Canto-II]

CANTO III

NEGOTIATIONS: HAIG MISSION

Even as the Task Force sails, Lord Carrington,
The Foreign Secretary resigns, accepting blame
For Britain's failure to prevent the invasion.
But in New York our envoy Anthony Parsons
Persuades the United Nations to resolve
That Argentina must instantly withdraw
Her forces from the Falklands. Within a week
Australia, Canada and New Zealand promise
Support for Britain's cause. While Tokyo nods
And Moscow holds back, West Germany and France
And by the weekend (the Easter holiday!)
All other EC states pledge to impose
Wide ranging sanctions against Argentina.
Buenos Aires is shocked by the severity
Of Europe's disapproval. Deeply in debt
(Mainly to Europe) the Junta is in dire straits
To raise further money to finance a war.

So far United States stays uncommitted
To Britain or Argentina, both her allies.
Conflicting views are voiced in Washington
About her rightful stance. Tom Enders thinks
Unites States' then-reviving influence
In Latin America should be reinforced
By backing Argentina. Jeane Kirkpatrick,
Washington's U.N. envoy glibly states
'If the islands are Argentina's no aggression
Has taken place'. But Alexander Haig,
The Secretary of State perceives the need
For U.S. to support her N.A.T.O. ally.

17

With Reagan's assent, Haig offers to mediate
Between the two antagonists in dispute.
London accepts, if Haig can first obtain
The Junta's compliance with Motion 502:
'Withdrawal of Argentine forces from the Falklands';
And to make public her determination
To repossess them, Britain designates
A naval exclusion zone around the Islands.

In London, new Foreign Secretary Pym
Assures Haig of his country's willingness
For talks, once Argentina withdraws her forces.
Till then Britain claims her right of self-defence
Under the U.N. Charter. Haig asks for room
For compromise in dealing with the Junta,
But recognises Britain's determined stance.

A cocksure mood prevails in Buenos Aires.
Huge demonstrations hailing the invasion
And hurling defiance at Britain greet Alex Haig.
The Junta considers this last response by Britain
Merely as bluffing. Radio and TV
Acclaim the occupation of the Malvinas
And scoff at Britain's resolve to repossess them.
A faint hint Argentina may withdraw,
Leaving clear evidence of her right to the Islands —
Provided the British Task Force sails back home —
Is all Haig can secure from Buenos Aires.

Once more in London, Haig secures from Pym
Promise that Britain might accept a form
Of joint administration of the Islands
Once Argentina's forces are withdrawn,
Though Pym stands firm on Whitehall's stipulation —
The Falklanders' right to self-determination.

Haig now reveals his own five-point solution:
Both British and Argentine forces to withdraw;
A three-flag interim administration;
Restored communications between Stanley
And Argentina; a long-term agreement
To be hammered out in talks; while balloting
The viewpoints of the Falkland Islanders.

18

Haig proffers his plan while cautioning the Junta:
'Comply with Resolution 502,
Or U.S.A. will give support to Britain.'
The Junta's in no temper for concessions.
Amaya is confident of victory;
His colleagues appear incapable of decisions.
Costa Mendez's alternative proposals
Find no acceptance by Britain. At this stage
Alex Haig brings his attempt to mediate to a halt.

M.P.s in Westminster grow more alarmed
As Britain'sTask Force steadily sails south.
The House had hoped settlement would follow
Once the Task Force had clearly demonstrated
Britain's resolution to retake the Falklands.
Labour demands talks through the United Nations
To reach a settlement. Even some Tory Members
Shrink from a shooting contest for the Islands.

A warlike Thatcher is prepared to fight
Though Pym prefers a more peaceable solution.
He flies to Washington with Whitehall's offer
Of interim joint rule (including U.S.)
Once Argentina's forces quit the Falklands.
Pym talks of Britain's need for U.S. assistance
But Haig finds little room for compromise
In Britain's attitude. Back home, Pym urges
Acceptance of Haig's plan but Thatcher objects.

The Royal Marines' attack upon South Georgia
Then taking place, steels Thatcher's resolution
To concede nothing over sovereignty.

To both parties Haig now sends his Final Package:
Phased joint withdrawal; interim oversight
By Britain, U.S.A. and Argentina;
Talks to explore, and agree within five years,
Terms to safeguard and ensure the interests
Of both the parties and the Falklanders.

Meanwhile Costa Mendez looks for support
Among his South American neighbour states
At the O.A.S.; in this he is rebuffed.
Argentina's arrogant outlook gives offence.
The Organisation merely calls for a truce
And for both sides to fulfil Clause 502.
Mendez asks Haig to clarify his proposals;
But Amaya, angry at losing South Georgia,
Charges the U.S. with duplicity.

So, Mendez rejects Haig's plan as falling short
Of Argentina's demands on sovereignty;
While Haig, now accepting the failure of his mission,
Informs his President, who thereupon
Imposes sanctions upon Argentina
And offers Britain military supplies.
Galtieri rages: 'I thought Reagan my friend!'
But Britain can now procure American missiles
And strategic secrets vital to her campaign.

Backed by U.S., Britain steps up her pressure.
A Total Exclusion Zone around the Falklands
Comes into force. From distant Ascension Island
A Vulcan bomber attacks Port Stanley's airfield,
Warning that Britain's intentions are in earnest.
Assured now as an ally, Pym flies to Haig
For U.S. help in seeking a solution
Through the United Nations. Thatcher, at last
Accepts that Britain should not be seen unwilling
To try for peace. With envoy Tony Parsons
Francis Pym hears Senor Perez de Cuellar,
United Nations Secretary General,
Outline his few 'ideas': first, withdrawal,
An interim administration, while awaiting
A long-term settlement. But this brief outline
Is overshadowed by a rival plan
Proposed by President Belaunde of Peru:

Haig's 'final package' with an added touch —
A Latin-American representative
To share the interim authority.

A third proposal made by David Owen,
Britain's former Foreign Secretary,
Calls for an Interim U.N. Trusteeship
Until a lasting settlement is forged.
In truth these new plans further cloud the issue
And diplomats find it difficult to gauge
Which formula offers their side most advantage.

[End of Canto-III]

CANTO IV

NAVAL DISASTERS : PLANS FOR LANDING

Royal Navy submarine *Splendid,* on patrol
North of the Falklands, locates enemy warships
Travelling south. A closer watch is ordered.
Submarine *Conqueror* is repaid with sightings
Of cruiser *Belgrano,* Argentine's flagship,
Escorted by destroyers. This major threat
To Britain's Task Force rouses 'Sandy' Woodward
To radio Admiral Fieldhouse at Northwood
To sanction an attack. The Cabinet
Examines all implications of such action:
The size and nature of the lurking danger
Belgrano poses; how such an attack
Outside the newly fixed Exclusion Zone
Corresponds with the rules of engagement;
The likely loss of lives, and injuries.
Lewin states openly the view of Northwood.
Belgrano, clearly a danger to the Task Force,
Should be destroyed. Its full review concluded,
The Cabinet agrees and gives its sanction.

Conqueror fires her torpedoes at *Belgrano.*
The second strikes astern, demolishing
Belgrano's power and communications,
Killing and maiming two hundred of her crew.
A raging fire, burning out of control
Traps men below, inflicting appalling burns.
The ship lists, sinking quickly. Captain Bonzo,
Powerless to save her, orders 'Abandon Ship!'
For thirty hours men drift in boats and life-rafts
Awaiting rescue. Three hundred and sixty perish.

This savage wreckage and massive loss of lives
Stuns world opinion. Men and women question
Our Navy's right to mete out such destruction,
To kill and maim so many. Support for Britain
In countries overseas is harshly jolted.
This ruthless act of war calls into question
The moral justification for her campaign.

Proposals for a peaceable solution
Put forward by De Cuellar and Belaunde
Break off. Yet this display of strength by Britain
Fails to deter her Argentine opponents.

Losing *Belgrano,* her country's much prized warship,
Arouses nation-wide fury in Argentina,
Which calls for immediate retaliation.
At such a moment concessions by the Junta
On Argentina's stand on sovereignty
Would constitute a major loss of face.
Galtieri therefore rejects Belaunde's plan —
Thus wrecking almost the last attempt at peace.

The Commons fear the Navy may have used
Unnecessary force to sink *Belgrano.*
Next day this mood is shattered. On patrol
North-east of Stanley, *Sheffield* is disabled —
Hit in her midst by an Exocet missile
Launched by an enemy Super Etendard.
Her hull is split, all power completely lost,
Broadcasting and fire-fighting gear destroyed.

Fire and smoke envelop decks surrounding
The engine room. Loss of mains-water foils attempts
To stop the spread of fire. As flames take hold,
Conditions in burning smoke-filled spaces worsen.
A desperate fight is made in breathing masks
Until the flames approach the magazine
Putting at risk the lives of the whole ship's crew.

With forty injured, many through burns and smoke,
And twenty-one men killed, Captain Salt orders
'Abandon Ship!' Fit men leap on to *Arrow,*
While injured men are quickly winched to safety
By helicopter. *Sheffield* floats for days,
But, sadly, under tow to a safe harbour,
This doughty ship rolls on her side and sinks.

The Task Force hears the news with disbelief.
The ease with which the enemy penetrated
Sheffield's defences almost without warning
Makes all too evident the deadly perils
Our sea-based Task Force risks daily in this conflict.

Woodward delivers a stern message to his fleet:
"We'll lose more ships, more men, but we shall win!"
Next day brings more bad news. Two Harriers
Believed to have collided, disappear.
A seventh of our fleet's air cover is now lost.
But from this juncture the Task Force becomes
More wary, alert, precise; each act declaring
Its single aim — the enemy's defeat.

As Britain again extends the Exclusion Zone
Nearer to Argentina, Admiral Woodward
Steps up his Force's pressure round the Falklands.
Submarines keep close watch for hostile aircraft
But no more enemy naval ships appear.
Harriers nightly harry enemy airfields.
Destroyer *Coventry* bombards the coast
Bringing down enemy aircraft with her Sea Darts.
Alacrity sinks an Argentine supply ship.
Brilliant, operating inshore with *Glasgow,*
Under severe attack shoots down three Skyhawks.
Such enemy raids, clearly guided to targets,
Throw suspicion on Argentine trawler *Narwhal*
Trailing the fleet despite orders to depart.
The ship is attacked and boarded; and from its crew,
A naval officer, discovered spying,
Is taken prisoner and transported home.

In secret, SAS and SBS
Ferret out enemy posts all round the Falklands.
Parties hide out on hills and landing sites
Observing the movements of an enemy
Half-trained, unhappy, chilled by wet and cold.
They note the strength and whereabouts of units
And placement of their weapons. Observation
Of natural features and obstacles to movement
Complete a picture of the enemy force
Then thought to number some ten thousand men.

A night reconnaisance on Pebble Island
Reveals an enemy garrison of one hundred
With many aircraft. Stealthily by night
D-Squadron SAS ably supported
By 148-Battery, 29-Commando,
Conveyed in Sea Kings, lands upon the Island
Swiftly destroying eleven enemy planes,
Withdrawing without loss. This well-planned raid
Rallies the spirits of the hard-pressed Task Force.

From intelligence collected, Thompson's planners
Search for the most advantageous landing site.
A plea for further troops has been accepted.
2-Para leaves home forthwith, with 5-Brigade
Preparing to join its comrades in the bridgehead.
Intrepid will furnish extra landing craft
And a helicopter base. The choice of beach-head
Will rest on ships on hand for the assault,
Hazards, and potential of the location,
And the likely strength of enemy resistance.
Steveley Bay is dropped as too remote.
Berkeley Sound near Port Stanley's too costly in aircraft
And, too exposed to aerial attack,
Is ruled out with reluctance. San Carlos Bay,
Although some fifty miles from Port Stanley
(Yet near an enemy vantage point at Darwin)
Provides protected anchorage for shipping.
Surveillance finds no enemy at San Carlos
Nor are mines found in the vicinity.

The sound advice of Ewen Southby-Tailyour
Assists the Task Force choice. Its presentation
Impresses the War Cabinet in London
And earns approval from Prime Minister Thatcher.
And now, the forward planning phase completed,
Thompson gives last instructions for a landing,
Awaiting the command — to go ahead.

Britain tries once again to reach agreement
By peaceful means. With Parsons from New York
The Cabinet presents its final package:
Both parties to withdraw; United Nations
To head an interim administration
With Argentine and British deputies.
Talks on the Falklands' future to be held
Without commitment and to be completed
By the year's end. New concessions by Britain
On interim rule and long-term governance
Place Argentina in a quandary.
To spurn proposals she has clamoured for
Will risk support she still holds in New York.
To play for time the Junta now insists
That both sides must withdraw to 'normal bases';
That interim rule under United Nations
Must exclude Britain, while still allowing
The Argentines free access to the islands.

This virtual rejection astonishes New York.
Kirkpatrick urges consent before too late,
But De Cuellar realises talks have run out of time.

In London Thatcher announces to the Commons:
Our peace attempts have failed. A white paper
Details Britain's vain efforts to reach agreement.
The Premier fiercely denounces Galtieri's
'Delay, obduracy, deception and bad faith'.
Concessions by Britain made in negotiations
Are all withdrawn. The order goes out to Woodward:
'Launch the planned operation at your discretion.'

[End of Canto-IV]

26

CANTO V

ASHORE AT SAN CARLOS : HEAVY AIR ATTACKS

The die is cast. In turn two thousand men
Waiting on lower decks of *Canberra*
Transfer by landing craft on to assault ships.
On crowded decks and gangways they kill time
Checking gear, reading or writing to their folks,
Queuing for meals served in the ship's packed galleys.
Maps are pored over, final briefings held,
As the assault ships with their naval escort
Cross the Exclusion Zone bound for San Carlos Bay.
Prayers for darkness, to avoid discovery,
Are answered. Unespied the convoy reaches
And slowly navigates the Falkland Sound.
At night assault troops eat a welcome meal,
Don their web fighting kit, blacken their faces,
Put helmets on, and rucksacks. In pitch darkness
They inch their way below to reach the tank decks
And clamber awkwardly into LCUs.

The mist has gone, leaving the flotilla
To steer a course charted by Southby-Tailyour
Through an alarmingly clear starlit night.
Gunfire to divert enemy attention
Away from our convoy punctuates the darkness.
Men shiver with cold and inactivity.
Some talk in subdued voices; most are silent,
Immersed in thoughts of what could lie ahead
But at this stage aware there's no way back.
Fear and discomfort blend to make them wish
To start the action and get it done with.

The LCUs touch ground near San Carlos beach.
2-Para wade in to the rocky shore,
Then start a long climb over marsh and stream
To the high summit of the Sussex mountains.
They reach this vital strongpoint unopposed.

North-east, 40-Commando's landing force
With Blues and Royals, Scorpions and Scimitars
Contact the Recce group of SBS.
Quickly securing first the beach-head zone
C-Company seeks local manager Pat Shore.
He greets them with delight. No Argentines
Are in the neighbourhood. Thankful Falklanders,
Shepherds and farm workers serve them with coffee.
Marines assume their planned defence positions
Facing towards Goose Green. As morning breaks,
The Union Jack is raised at Pat Shore's house.
By night this sight is flashed around the globe!

That night a raiding force of SBS
Attacks an enemy post near Fanning Head
Which guards the entrance to San Carlos Water.
Dropped miles away they toil across the headland
To train a barrage of machine-gun fire
Against the enemy. A naval salvo
From frigate *Antrim* strengthens the attack.
The Argentines retreat. Captain Rod Bell's
Yells for surrender vanish in high winds.
A further barrage is fired, until at dawn,
The post is captured with nine prisoners.
More men had escaped, but the guns are silenced.

Across the waterway, 45-Commando
Seizes the disused refrigeration plant
At Ajax Bay, and mans the heights above.
Finally, after night delays, 3-Paras
Disembark in daylight at Port San Carlos.
The coastline now secured, Britain's assault fleet
Move to their anchorage in San Carlos Water.

So with one lucky, well-planned operation
Commando Brigade at last secures a land base.
Their first goal thus achieved, the Force begins
Its main task — to expel the enemy.

While our troops urgently begin
The vital task of settling in
Argentina spotters soon report
Ship movements in San Carlos Port.
Landing craft quickly rush ashore
Supplies essential for the war.
Sea Kings on their day's first flights
Hoist Rapier launchers to hilltop sites.
Signallers work with frantic haste
Establishing a radio base.
On beaches piled with combat gear
Men toil like ants to keep them clear.
Falklanders, glad to lend a hand
Fetch tractors to drive stores inland.
Yet the whole bridgehead is aware
Of fearful danger from the air —
Danger for which all now prepare.

Even as they land at Port San Carlos
3-Para espy a group of Argentines
Retreating at speed. They hasten them with fire.
Unhappily a Sea King helicopter
Transporting goods, convoyed by two Gazelles
Is seen and fired at by the enemy
Who shoot down both Gazelles, killing three airmen.

The enemy now launches a strong attack,
Our troops replying with the utmost vigour.
Pucaras strafing Paras on Sussex mountains
Are hit by Stinger missiles. A bomb attack
By Aeromacchi on transport *Fort Austin*
Misfires. Rockets encircling *Argonaut*
Fall wide, but cannon-fire wrecks her radar
And wounds three crewmen.

Thenceforth throughout the day enemy aircraft
Strafe the whole fleet with rockets, bombs and cannons.
Mirage and Skyhawks launch repeated raids
At zero feet, eluding radar screens,
And hidden by hills, are lost within split seconds.

To counter enemy long-range combat aircraft
Our Harriers patrol the islands ceaselessly
Guided by sight or radar from our ships.
A Chinook and a Puma are brought down
By cannon fire. Above San Carlos Water
Two Harriers attack a wave of Skyhawks,
Shooting down four. The same day Harrier pilots
Morell and Leery, launching Sidewinder,
And using cannon-fire, shoot down two more.

Right from the start, our pilots recognise
The capabilities of Mirage and Skyhawk.
But with the Harriers' superb acceleration
And piloted by Britain's finest airmen
Launching with deadly aim Sidewinder missiles,
Enemy raiders are blasted from the sky.
Yet Task Force airmen are severely hampered
By ineffective early warning radar.
Enemy planes flying at near sea level
Escape detection on our radar screens
Until almost on target. Repeatedly
The enemy strafe their targets, while our planes
Can only spot them on their homeward flights.
And yet our pilots, though so few in number,
On Day-1 fight with seventy enemy planes.

The enemy now concentrates his aim
Upon our shipping round the Falklands coasts.
Under attack, *Antrim* replies with Sea Slugs
Just as bombs strike her magazine, destroying
Her missile system and rendering the ship
Hors de combat. Throughout the day
Norland and *Canberra* (both vital targets)
Endure intense attack with fortitude.

Argentine airmen show amazing courage
In pressing home attacks upon our shipping,
Defying Sea Cats, Rapiers and Blowpipe.
A hit puts *Brilliant's* Sea Wolf out of action.
Crewmen are wounded in attacks on *Broadsword*
Before her Sea Wolf scores a direct hit
On a marauding Mirage. Ground atmospherics
Badly distort our radar tracking signals,
Forcing our crews to aim by lines of sight.

As *Argonaut* replaces damaged *Antrim*
Outside San Carlos, Skyhawks attack in force.
With Sea Cat, *Argonaut* destroys one aircraft
But six more loose their bombs at near mast level.
Though most fall harmlessly into the sea
One bomb destroys a boiler which explodes,
Extinguishing the frigate's steam supply.
A second hits the Sea Cat magazine.
Missile explosions kill the magazine crew,
Yet bombs which cause them fail to explode.
With one Sea Cat still firing, *Argonaut*
Is towed by *Plymouth* to San Carlos Water
For close inspection and necessary repair.

Ill fortune allows a final blow to smite
The Task Force on this catastrophic day.
Ardent, struck first by thousand-pounder bombs
That wreck her vital systems, then receives
Renewed attack that sets the ship on fire,
Killing and wounding more than fifty men.
Gallant resistance by machine-gun teams
Fails to save *Ardent*. Her surviving crew
Are rescued from the sea and burning frigate
By helicopter and by warship *Yarmouth*.
That evening medical teams aboard *Canberra*
Start the long task of caring for the wounded
As the campaign gets under way in earnest.

By night Navy Command reviews the day.
One frigate sunk, four seriously damaged,
Defences overwhelmed by hostile aircraft;
Yet fear of missiles makes them fly so low
That their attacks are often ineffective.
Rapier missiles, relied on for fleet protection
Have little success. Quite rightly 'Sandy' Woodward
Demands improvement. But enemy air losses,
Reckoned at twenty, must surely be too high.
This slender hope serves to console our Staff.

[End of Canto-V]

CANTO VI

RENEWED AIR BATTLES : FURTHER SHIP LOSSES

The parlous situation of the Task Force
Calls for immediate action. A day's respite
From air attack, while the enemy regroups
His squadrons, lets our commanders re-deploy
Our units most at risk. Liner *Canberra,*
Most valuable target for hostile aircraft,
Flanked by supply and other non-combat ships
Is convoyed eastwards out of enemy range.
Glamorgan takes the place of damaged *Antrim*
On escort duty. Repairs to *Argonaut*
Are stopped by loss of power. R.E.s defuse
One unexploded bomb but cannot reach
A second, so the ship is towed to safety.
A surgical team locates its Field Hospital
At Ajax Bay refrigeration plant
With maintenance and equipment stores nearby;
While to reduce the risk of air attack,
Movements of stores by day are all forbidden.
The ban gravely hinders 3-Commando Brigade
In speeding its battle group's build-up ashore.

Enemy aircraft reappear next day. At once
The air battle resumes with varying fortunes.
While Harriers destroy three helicopters,
A British Lynx hits an Argentine freighter
Forcing another aground. Dive-bombing our warships,
Three Mirages are brought down in the sea.
Skyhawks then attack *Antelope* and *Broadsword.*
One plane is hit, just as a bomb strikes *Broadsword*
Without exploding. A second aircraft,
Peppered by cannon as it dives to bomb,
Crashes on *Antelope* and disintegrates.

Its bomb lands the same moment. A second bomb
From another aircraft hits the engine room
But neither explodes. Phillips and Prescott,
Bomb disposal experts with nerves of steel
Work to defuse them; but sadly Phillips, cast
In heroic mould, is killed as one bomb explodes.
Fire spreads throughout the ship. Boats from the fleet
Surround the *Antelope,* barely in time
To save her crew. Her magazine explodes,
Rocking the anchorage as the ship breaks up.
She sinks next day, her grim fate bringing home
The bitter harvest of the Falklands War.

The Admiral takes counsel with his captains
By telephone. In sombre mood they urge him
To move the carriers closer to the action
To give the Harriers longer in the air
Over the combat zone. This would provide
An extra combat team to stay on watch
To halt the enemy *en route* to his target.
Woodward believes the risk is far too great.
To lose either *Invincible* or *Hermes*
Would mean disaster. Losses of ships to date
Showing the enemy's skill and striking power
Compel the commander to avoid such risks.
But operating from a base at sea
Thus lengthening all journeys to and fro
Bedevils the logistics of supply.
Fuel used on lengthy journeys drains reserves.
Ship movements at night only, decrease the flow
Of stores and weapons needed to enable
The battle group to launch its land campaign.
Helicopters, fully in use to move supplies,
Cannot be detailed for combat support.
While the supply stockpile on shore progresses,
Rival demands for limited means of transport,
Insufficient to provide for all the needs
Of Britain's naval and land force commands,
Create untimely strains in their relations.

Next day Skyhawks attack two landing ships —
Sir Galahad and *Sir Lancelot* with bombs.
Though none explodes, both vessels are withdrawn
For closer examination by bomb experts.
Thus though intact, both are put out of action.

This day our air defence is more successful.
Rapier crews, fast growing more accurate,
Destroy three hostile planes from hilltop sites.
Fearless shoots down two aircraft with her Bofors,
While Auld and Smith, patrolling in Harriers,
Confront four Mirages, destroying three
Using Sidewinder missiles.
               Throughout the conflict
The Task Force squadrons lose no planes in action —
Just four in accidents and three from ground fire.
Pilots are often utterly exhausted
After their daily stints of constant sorties
From dawn to dusk, with night alerts by rota;
Churchill himself would have been the first to praise
This dedicated body of high-flyers!

The loss of planes suffered by Argentina
Appals their air command, keen to maintain
The spirits of their inexperienced pilots.
But hostile air defences round San Carlos,
With Harriers growing daily more effective,
Demoralise the waves of enemy raiders
Who turn away before they reach their targets.
From now the tide of battle starts to turn.

The Task Force braces itself for an all-out assault
On May 25th, Argentina's National Day.
Attacks by enemy aircraft are intense
But air defence is fierce. Sea Dart missiles
From *Coventry* bring down three Mirages.
Yarmouth and Rapiers destroy two more.

(May 25)
COVENTRY
●

Pebble
Isla

Saunders Island

Byron Sound

WEST FALKLAND

King George Bay

Swan Island

Queen Charlotte Bay

Fox Bay

Weddell Island

WEST
FALKLAND

Falkland Sound

Speedwell Island

George Island

ARGENTINA

SOUTH ATLANTIC

Falkland Islands

BELGRANO
(May 2)
●

MAP OF TH

OCEAN

Cow Bay

North Falkland Sound

Douglas Settlement

Teal Inlet

(May 24)
TELOPE

May 21)
RDENT ●

San Carlos Water

Port San Carlos

Berkeley Sound

Teal Inlet Settlement

Top Maio House

Estancia House

Mt Low

Mt Longdon

San Carlos

Grantham

Sussex Mts

EAST FALKLAND

Mt Kent

Moody Brook

Two Sisters

Tumbledown

○ STANLEY

nd Sound

Sapper Hill

Camilla Creek House

Fitzroy Settlement

Bluff Cove Settlement

Darwin

(June 8) SIR GALAHAD

Goose Green
Settlement

Choiseul Sound

Swan Inlet

LAFONIA

Lively Island

Low Bay

7 Bay of Harbours

Sea Lion Islands

ALKLANDS

37

Raids are contained until, near Pebble Island,
Coventry is alerted. Attacking Skyhawks
Swinging aside from concentrated gun-fire
Let loose at *Broadsword.* A bomb pierces her side,
Destroys a helicopter and bounces out
Without exploding. *Broadsword's* Sea Wolf takes aim
At Skyhawks, just at the instant *Coventry* turns
To narrow her target; so Sea Wolf cannot fire.
Four bombs hit *Coventry's* side and detonate
Wrecking her power and transmission systems.
Her engine room explodes, killing nine men.
Fire sweeps the ship, causing horrific burns.
The ship lists badly. Men jump overboard
Taking to life-rafts. Hardly conscious,
Captain Hart-Dyke is helped into a raft
That soon capsizes and is washed away.
With more survivors he is winched to safety
By helicopter, but nineteen die in all.
Suffering severe cold, the rescued men
Are ferried to supply vessel *Fort Austin*
For ultimate trans-shipment home to Britain.
This new disaster, casting doubt upon
Our missiles' power to home in and destroy
Enemy missiles with trails diffused by cold
Alarms the Force — but more trouble is to come.

Two Super Etendards on special missions
To inflict maximum damage on our shipping
Attack the fleet carrying Exocet missiles.
Ambuscade detects trails on her radar
And warns the fleet. She fires with all her weapons
Including chaff decoys. The missile veers
Away from warships to a new course, and hits
Atlantic Conveyor, Task Force container ship,
Not armed with chaff. The Exocet explodes
Setting the ship on fire. *Ambuscade*
With other frigates helps to save survivors.
Unluckily her helicopter-load,
Earmarked for transport to our Landing Force
This very night, is left as blazing ruins.

Most of the crew leap overboard to life-rafts
But Ian North, the master, 'Captain Birdseye',
With eleven more men is sadly lost at sea.
Loss of the Chinooks to move troops into place
Ready to make a breakout from the beach-head,
Delayed till now by overdue supplies,
Further disrupts the Commandos' forward plans.

Enemy planes keep up destructive raids.
Skyhawks launch an attack on Ajax Bay,
Setting the main munitions dump on fire
While badly damaging the Field Hospital.
Exploding shells and mortars spread destruction.
Six men are killed; twenty-seven are wounded.
Power is lost and survivors comb the wreckage
To find and help the wounded in the dark.
Two unexploded bombs, a metre long,
Lodged in the walls of the vast Dressing Station
Make it a death trap. Space around is cleared,
The bombs are enclosed within a screen of sandbags;
Yet with no replacement premises at hand,
Treatment of wounds and urgent surgery
Continue there amid the devastation.
Other sites are explored, without result.
So, the Field Hospital stays at Ajax Bay,
The bombs, unwanted neighbours, lying there,
Until the end.

British fortunes are at their lowest ebb.
Losses of ships and planes severely damage
Our prospect of victory. These latest sinkings
Make Admiral Woodward take still greater care
To place his carriers well beyond the reach
Of enemy aircraft; by this act increasing
The army's formidable logistics problems.

Yet from the lowest point one can but rise.
From this time onward enemy aircraft raids,
Save for one final desperate assault,
Are limited to hit-and-run attacks.

Losses of aircraft and experienced pilots
Are on a scale Argentina can sustain
No longer. Powerful Task Force defences
Around San Carlos finally achieve
Partial superiority in the skies
Above the Falklands; in time to support
The Army's battle to regain the Islands.

London waits eagerly for first reports
Of troop advances from San Carlos Bay.
News of air battles with disastrous loss
And damage to so many of our ships
Creates a mood of gloom and indignation
Back home in Britain. News about the conflict,
Both good and bad, is told in churchyard tones
By the Ministry of Defence. The lurking dangers
To men and shipping in the Falklands zone
Torment the nation. Everyone is concerned
That the campaign should speedily be ended,
And longs for quick successes — none more so
Than Britain's Cabinet; not wholly grasping
Our Land Force's logistic handicaps —
Merely awaiting favourable news
To cheer an anxious Parliament and people.

By phone Northwood conveys the Cabinet's view
To Brigadier Thompson. Britain's Landing Force
Should launch an attack forthwith against Goose Green,
The enemy's strongpoint south of Port San Carlos.
Thompson objects: Goose Green can be contained
And dealt with later. The Brigadier's plan,
A push inland in strength to take Mount Kent,
High vantage point from which to attack Port Stanley,
Gains support from Northwood; which nonetheless —
Asked by the Cabinet for quick results —
Decrees an immediate strike against Goose Green.

Thompson gives instant orders to his commanders:
2-Para to occupy Darwin and Goose Green;
3-Para and 45-Commando to advance
Inland towards Teal Inlet by forced marches.

[End of Canto-VI]

40

FALKLANDS VICTORY:

CANTO VII
DARWIN AND GOOSE GREEN

Plans for 2-Para's thrust towards Goose Green
Are settled at Brigade San Carlos 'O' Group.
Logistics constraints hamper the operation.
Artillery support is limited
To three 105-millimeter guns
For lack of helicopters to move more forward.
Shortage of fuel rules out light tank support.
Soft marshy ground, likewise prevents the use
Of tracked BVs to carry heavy weapons.
Only two mortars, humped by men, are carried,
But *Arrow* gives gun support from Falkland Sound.

Tired of inaction in the cold and wet,
2-Para begins advancing south at dusk,
Weighed down with arctic rations and equipment
Through rocks and marsh; D-Company in the lead
Cautiously pushing ahead on cratered ground.
Their first objective — Camilla Creek House —
Is made secure. Colonel Jones tells his men
To use the house as shelter for the night.

Dawn shows the Paras resting in a hollow,
Safe from all but a close-up aerial view,
Well hidden from enemy spotters until nightfall.
In sheer disbelief they hear BBC's World Service
Announce: '2-Para is approaching Darwin'.
Enraged, the Colonel orders his battalion:
'Disperse and dig in; prepare for an attack
By air or gun-fire'. The enemy, forewarned,
Flies in more troops to Darwin and Goose Green.
The Colonel outlines his plans: C-Company
Will hold the start line. Meanwhile A and B
Will push down east and west sides of the isthmus.

D-Company will then advance through B.
C-Company's advance begun in rain,
Is led by 59-Squadron Engineers
Who work waist-deep in water in the darkness
To clear bridges of mines. A-Company
Crosses the start line early after midnight
Towards its first objective, Burntside House.
As they advance, the enemy opens fire.
Paras reply with machine-guns and grenades.
Two Argentines are killed; the others fly.
Amazingly, civilians, men and women,
Are found in the house, unhurt though terrified.

B-Company destroys a machine-gun post
Soon after starting. In their movement south,
Meeting with well-defended enemy strongpoints
Paras react with courage, dash and coolness,
Clearing them one by one. But advance is slowed
When *Arrow's* gun is jammed, reducing their firepower.

A-Company moves forward unopposed
To Coronation Point, near to Darwin.
While enemy positions in the rear
Are being cleared by D-Company,
The signal to advance towards the town
Is made. In growing daylight, A-Company
Runs into enemy entrenched positions.
Intense artillery and mortar fire
Now harass paratroops throughout the isthmus.
Heavy machine-guns rake A-Company,
Not armed with a sufficient weight of fire
To quell the enemy's massive bombardment.
Platoon No. 1 gets pinned down in the open,
Its men escaping at intervals through smoke,
But Engineer Corporal Melia is killed.
Privates Tuffin and Worrall are both wounded.
Corporals Abols and Prior bring Tuffin in
When Prior is hit. Corporal Hardman helps Abols
But luckless Prior is hit again and killed.

Abols and Hardman go back once again
To pick up Worrall; such are the selfless acts
Of routine courage that took place that day.

B-Company is equally hard pressed.
Major Crosland's advance on enemy posts
Near Boca House with Platoons Four and Six
Is interrupted by well-placed machine-guns.
But Platoon Five, providing fire for cover,
Suffers three wounded while regaining dead ground.
Private Illingworth, bearing an injured man,
Is shot dead by a sniper. The lead platoon
Is pinned down on the ridge by Boca House.
Insufficient firepower and ammunition
Defeat 2-Para's resolute attempts
To quieten the enemy's machine-guns.
His guns and mortars sweep across our lines
Without a pause. Yet enemy Pucaras
Attack, but turn away from their reception.
Our gunners strive to keep their weapons firing
As gun trails bury themselves in the soft ground;
But naval gun support is now withdrawn;
And *Arrow,* thought too great a risk at sea
In day light, is recalled to San Carlos Water.

Colonel Jones comes to talk with Farrar-Hockley.
Well-placed machine-guns blast the open ground
Around the Paras. To break this stranglehold
Strong enemy positions must be taken.
The Major leads a party up the hillside
Through heavy fire. In minutes Captain Dent,
His 2-i-C, the Adjutant Captain Wood,
And Corporal Hardman all are shot and killed.

Caught in a hail of fire, the party withdraws
To less open ground. Meanwhile Colonel 'H' Jones,
Armed with a sub-machine gun leads a small group
Around a spur to attack a machine-gun post.
Advancing while firing, 'H' comes under fire
From enemy posts behind him. Warned too late
The Colonel falls, machine-gunned from behind.

In minutes, three officers and nine men have been lost.
But loss of their comrades animates our men
With a new-found spirit. Well-aimed machine-gun fire
And '66' rockets silence enemy trenches.
Brave men risk death to clear destructive bunkers.
White flags are flown. Artillery and mortars
Still pound A-Company, but resistance ebbs
And enemy soldiers come out to surrender.
These well-defended Darwin Hill positions
Have been secured with seventy prisoners.

The gravely wounded Colonel does not rally
And dies with Farrar-Hockley at his side.
The Major signals Keeble, 2-i-C
To Colonel Jones, telling him of the news
And urging him to the spot to take command.

The Paras mourn their Colonel — no man braver!
Reckless? His whole attack in jeopardy
From lethal fire raking A-Company,
'H' Jones's timely charge inspired his men
To feats undreamed of, transforming defeat
To hard won victory. Paras and Goose Green
Are names the Argentines do not forget,
Which hasten their ultimate surrender.
For outstanding personal leadership and courage
Colonel Jones was awarded a posthumous V.C.

With many casualties, A-Company
Badly needs helicopters for its wounded.
By ill luck the first to approach them is shot down,
Its pilot killed when nearing the location.
Others arrive with Captain Hughes, M.D.,
Who treats the severest cases on the spot.
Then while A-Company's wounded are air-lifted
Injured prisoners are given treatment
Before being transported back to base.

44

Major Keeble, 2-Para's acting commander,
Reviews the battle state. A-Company,
Its goal secured, is mopping up and resting.
B-Company's attack on Boca House
Meets strong resistance. Extra weight of fire
Is urgently required to overcome it.
D-Company's Milan crews and machine-guns
Sent forward by Colonel Jones to lend support
Are grouped to train their fire on enemy bunkers.

As D-Company sets out along the shore
Hidden by cliffs, to turn the enemy's flank,
Keeble unleashes a massed concentration
Of fire-power from the ridge. Still under fire
Our machine-gunners sustain more injuries;
But Milan rockets score two direct hits
On enemy positions. From the shore
D-Company advances up the hillside
Raking the enemy with flanking fire.
Tired and shocked, Argentines now begin
Emerging from their dug-outs to surrender.
Bunkers are cleared, prisoners are rounded up,
Wounded attended to. With Boca House
A major strongpoint seized, the way is clear
For an advance on Darwin and Goose Green.

Keen to maintain momentum, Major Keeble
Orders the Paras forward without delay.
Thus while C-Company clears Darwin Hill,
Patrols take over Darwin settlement
Rooting out its defenders.
                              Further south:
Artillery, mortars and machine-gun fire
Rain down on Paras as they work their way
Towards Goose Green through ground with little cover.
B-Company sweeps wide around the airfield
To strike from the south-west; while C and D
Make a combined attack on Goose Green schoolhouse.

The enemy fights back strongly till at last
A white flag is flown. D-Company's Jim Barry
Advances to take surrender, but is shot dead.
The angry Paras rake the place with gun-fire
And no defender lives through the attack.

As D-Company resumes its forward movement
Two Skyhawks drop bombs far too close for comfort.
Moments later, Pucaras launch an attack
With rockets and napalm; the blazing jelly
Drops wide, just when a Blowpipe missile launcher
Destroys a Pucara. Fuel from its tanks
Soaks a whole section, luckily without harm,
While small-arms fire brings down a second aircraft.

At length Paras find relief when Harriers
Attack and wipe out enemy gun positions
That harass every movement of our men.
By night the now-surrounded enemy
Slackens his fire but still has power to threaten
The tired British. Enemy helicopters
Are seen landing reinforcements near Goose Green.
Keeble bombards the area with gun-fire
Preventing several machines from landing.
No attack follows. Victory is near
But at a cost. The Paras are near exhaustion,
Their ammunition low.

By radio Keeble asks for reinforcements,
Weapons and ammunition, with helicopters
To ferry out the many dead and wounded.
He hopes to take Goose Green without a battle
And calls for an intense artillery barrage
On enemy positions. Early next day
Two prisoners are taken to the ridge line
With letters for the Argentine Commander
Asking for the safe passage of civilians
And calling for his forces to surrender.

Pedroza, conscious of his nation's honour,
Consults his C-in-C General Menendez
Who gives him leave to act as he thinks fit.

Pedroza's force, one hundred and fifty strong,
Members of Argentina's vaunted Air Force,
Form up and surrender; but more men then appear,
Relieved to escape the Paras'lethal onslaught.
Nine hundred men of Argentina's Army
Commanded by Lieutenent-Colonel Pioggi
Surrender to 2-Para's D-Company.
Thus ends the first phase of the Falklands land war.

In one tough fight 2-Para had defeated
A force four times its size, had reached its goals —
All by bold action and at far less expense
To either combatant than had been feared.

Now, a brief spell to rest, refit, take stock.
Paras meet Falklanders and hear accounts
Of their captivity. At Ajax Bay
In crude surroundings, Field Hospital staff
With dedicated skill care for the wounded.
Finally, beside San Carlos Waters,
With simple ceremony, Padre Cooper
Honours and buries 2-Para's battle victims
Whose gallant conduct in a bitter conflict
Throws lustre on this hard-won victory.

[End of Canto-VII]

FALKLANDS VICTORY:

CANTO VIII

ADVANCES BY LAND AND SEA : FITZROY DISASTER

Through streams and marshes, over hills, in rain
45-Commandos foot-slog towards Mount Kent,
Each man weighed down with arms and ammunition;
BVs — their baggage transport — following
With heavy weapons, wireless kit and stragglers.
Their clothing soaked, webbing stiff on their shoulders,
The hills devoid of trees, with little wildlife;
And but for rare pleasing views of creeks and hillsides,
Lacking the rugged charms of Wales or Scotland.

The long cold nights fail to uplift their spirits.
Strained limbs and ankles, sore and blistered feet
Afflict too many. Hard pressed NCOs,
Footsore themselves, daily spur on their men
To further effort; while keeping careful watch
Against a likely enemy attack.
At Douglas Station, farming settlement,
45-Commandos find only Falklanders;
An enemy force had left the day before.
Men pause to rest their feet and dry their footwear,
Then resume their march at speed for Teal Inlet.

3-Para, moving ahead of 45-Commando,
March from Teal Inlet to Estancia House,
A group of farmsteads neighbouring Mount Kent.
Here, D-Squadron SAS, already on watch,
Has cleared Kent's slopes of enemy patrols
And thinks the summit only lightly held.
Well aware of its tactical importance,
Thompson decides to seize the Mount forthwith.
Sea Kings airlift men of K-Company
(42-Commando) to act with the SAS.

Heavily overloaded, skimming hilltops,
Traversing terrain still in enemy hands,
Wearing night goggles, flying in fading light
Our pilots display superlative skill
In landing their Sea Kings, while the SAS
Fights off another Argentine patrol.

K-Company, scaling Mount Kent's steep slopes
Finds the peak undefended. Through the night
Numbed by the cold, the party waits for daylight
And likely air attack. The sole Chinook
Spared from *Atlantic Conveyor's* calamity
Flies in three 105-guns as support.

At daybreak Colonels Rose and Vaux, Commanders
Of SAS Squadrons and 42-Commando
Gaze on the distant view of Moody Brook,
Argentine Army base fronting Port Stanley
With sheer excitement. At last our troops command
The heights from which to dominate the land war.

The battle for the hills gathers momentum.
At night detachments of 42-Commando
Flown in by Sea Kings seize Mount Challenger.
3-Para holds Mounts Estancia and Vernet.
The SAS is secure on Murrell Heights.
Its patrols bring in four captives and discover
Enemy strongposts recently abandoned.

45-Commando completes its epic march
And occupies the rear slopes of Mount Kent.
3-Commando Brigade at last is poised
To seize Port Stanley; anxious to attack
Now that continual cold and wet conditions
Begin to prevail. Threatened mist, ice and gales
Would slow our forces in their final thrusts
And prejudice an early victory.

Immediate attack is therefore vital.

Now, let us travel back some weeks in time,
And back to Britain where 5-Brigade, composed
Of Welsh Guards, Scots Guards and of Gurkha Rifles
Is warned for Falklands duty. To prepare,
It holds a full-scale exercise in Brecon
Simulating conditions in the Falklands.
Its fitting out is dogged by shortages,
With combat equipment, field artillery,
Clothing and transport all in short supply;
Its voyage south in stripped down luxury
In liner *QE2* is yet in marked contrast
With harsh conditions prevailing in the Falklands.

At Ascension, General Moore joins *QE2*
En-route to take command of Falklands Land Force.
At South Georgia the regiments are transferred
To *Canberra* and *Norland*. Jeremy Moore
Now boards command ship *Fearless* in Carlos Waters
Relieving Julian Thompson of his command.
In circumstamces where combat decisions
Were subject to political control,
Thompson's feats in landing the British Land Force,
Holding a beach-head despite continued assaults,
And launching stubborn attacks towards Port Stanley
Are operations he can recall with pride.

General Moore draws on experience
His troops had gained so far in operations.
With Brigadier Wilson he surveys the scene
And plans forthcoming action. Fresh from home
Wilson wants 5-Brigade to win its spurs
By striking towards Port Stanley from the south
Rather than backing 3-Brigade's advance.
Moore gives consent. 2-Para at Goose Green
Is placed in Wilson's command. His 5-Brigade
Will push for Stanley via Bluff Cove and Fitzroy.
But once again a lack of helicopters
Holds up the plan. Supplies for 3-Brigade
Dispersed between Teal Inlet and Mount Kent
Demand priority. All transport planes
Are used to ferry stores to Teal Inlet
As 5-Brigade begins to come ashore.

The Gurkhas, landing at San Carlos Water
Start marching to Goose Green without delay.
Here, Wilson for the first time meets 2-Para.
His planned advance to Bluff Cove via the coast road
By infantry, using 2-Para as screen,
Is judged impractical. 2-Para staff
Pass on the word that Falklanders believe
A phone-link from Swan Inlet on to Fitzroy
May still exist. A swift raid on Swan Inlet
Might furnish worthwhile news. Wilson approves.
A helicopter recce to Swan Inlet
Finds it deserted. A phone-call raises Fitzroy,
Whose manager reports that Argentines
Have blown up Bluff Cove bridge and left in haste.

At this news Wilson delegates 2-Para
To fly by Chinook to investigate.
A-company seizes high ground near Bluff Cove.
B-Company follows. Patrols sent out
Confirm the area clear of enemy.
Platoons deploy and begin digging in.
Moore's HQ does not totally approve.
By thus extending lines of communication
Beyond the range of British guns and aircraft
5-Brigade is open to ground or air attack.
Guns and supplies are moved up through the night
To strengthen the Paras. The quick dash to Bluff Cove
Impels the need to consolidate the ground
Won in the move. Wilson believes he has saved
Much time and fighting. Now the urgent need
Is to concentrate units of 5-Brigade
Around 2-Para. Gurkhas are on patrol
Combing Lafonia for enemy stragglers.
The Guards regiments are landing in Carlos Bay.
At once Welsh Guards begin to march to Goose Green;
But newly arrived, not yet acclimatised
And lacking adequate supporting transport,
They set out too weighed down. In the conditions
The march is stopped and Guards return to Carlos.

A second plan, to move the Guards by sea,
Is studied and agreed. At night, Scots Guards
Embark on ship *Intrepid,* then transfer
Off Lively Island on to landing craft
Commanded by Major Ewen Southby-Tailyour.
In storm conditions, his radar rendered useless,
Skirting a jagged coast in heavy seas,
Finding Bluff Cove becomes a seaman's nightmare.

Southby-Tailyour's skill in navigation
Is tested to the limit. Troubles worsen
When a British frigate shells the craft in error.
After a night of unrelieved rough weather,
Exhausted Guardsmen come ashore at daybreak —
Wet through, some even suffering from exposure.
At length they take up posts held for some days
By 2- Para, also drenched and short of food,
Who gladly retire to Fitzroy to dry out.

Intrepid returns to Carlos at full speed
To reach the anchorage before first light.
Word of an Exocet launcher based ashore
Alarms the Navy, under heavy pressure
From Northwood to move all of 5-Brigade
To forward combat areas by sea.
A further attempt by assault ship is agreed.
Welsh Guards embark on *Fearless* to transfer
To landing craft at night, this time off Fitzroy.
Atrocious weather makes it impossible
To launch the landing craft. With daylight near,
Fearless offloads two companies of Guardsmen
To reach the shore in her own LCUs
While *Fearless* makes the journey back to Carlos
With three hundred more Welsh Guardsmen still aboard.

But now the Navy makes a firm decision.
Capital ships no longer may be risked
On chancy ventures. Whitehall cannot sustain
The possibility of a major loss.
Open sea moves must be made by landing ships.

Unheralded, without escort, landing ship *Tristram*
Reaches Bluff Cove, laden with ammunition.
The beach party ashore starts to offload her
Without air cover or local ground defence.
Moreover Fitzroy, Britain's most forward land base
Lacks any signals-link from ship to shore
Or links with Navy HQ at San Carlos.
A landing ship sails post-haste to Goose Green
To bring essential signals-gear and transport.

At dawn the landing ship *Sir Galahad*
Arrives off Fitzroy carrying more Welsh Guardsmen.
Conflicting orders have delayed its passage.
Horrified by the ship's exposed position
Out in the bay in daylight, Southby-Tailyour
Borrows a landing craft half-filled with ammo
To bring the Guards ashore without delay.

The Guards decline to travel with munitions
(—A risk forbidden by Army Regulations).
Crass though S-T considers their objection,
No other boat can land them right away.
Harrier patrols by now extend their flights
Near to their limit to give Fitzroy air cover.
At noon, control sends them an urgent call
To protect *Plymouth,* bombing off West Falkland,
From imminent attack. Untimely switch!
Within a brief space Skyhawks and Mirages
Descend on Fitzroy, unchecked by British planes.

Bombs on *Sir Galahad* start petrol fires,
Killing and causing fearful burns to Guardsmen,
Who, dazed and still on fire, stagger to life-rafts.
Sir Tristram, also hit, fires at the raiders
While launching boats to help *Sir Galahad.*
All available helicopters are used
To rush the many badly injured Guardsmen
For medical care at Ajax Bay and Carlos.

Plymouth, under attack by five Mirages
Accounts for two with Oerlikon and Sea Cats;
Then four huge bombs cause fires and devastation.
The ship limps back into San Carlos Water
To douse her fires and remedy the damage.

A later enemy bombing raid on Fitzroy
Meets hostile small-arms fire and turns away.
Along the coast the planes meet *Foxtrot-4,*
Back from Goose Green with signals-gear and transport:
Despite strict orders, travelling back in daylight.
The planes attack, causing extensive damage
And killing Sergeant Johnston and five others.
Coaster *Monsoonum* rescues her survivors
But *Foxtrot-4* sinks quickly under tow.

Thus Britain loses thirty-three Welsh Guardsmen,
Seven Royal Navy men, six merchant seamen,
Five other soldiers killed; more than forty wounded
And badly burned, all in a single day.
Ships and transport, with vital gear, are lost.
Our sole riposte — four enemy planes shot down.
So, on a day of unrelieved misfortune,
Reeling under the shock of the Fitzroy disaster
The Task Force comes to terms with its fearful lessons
Bitterly learnt with pain and loss of life.

[End of Canto-VIII]

FALKLANDS VICTORY:

CANTO IX

THE MOUNTAIN WAR : *GLAMORGAN* DAMAGED

In Britain, these reverses cause consternation.
News of the heavy toll of dead and injured
Horrifies families of servicemen.
Buenos Aires announces that British losses
Are on a scale to halt an attack on Stanley.
Moore asks Whitehall to keep this belief alive
By not releasing the names of casualties.
At home the M.O.D. withstands intense pressure
From relatives, anguished by this news black-out,
To publish them. John Nott prevaricates,
Hinting this would assist the enemy
And holds back names till Stanley is assaulted.

The Fitzroy mishap betrays the diverse views
Held by Task Force Command and Correspondents
On the release of news about the conflict.
The Force's instinct is to withhold all news
That might endanger men, machines or ships
Or compromise its future strategy.
For their part, Correspondents see their role
As reporting fully news of the campaign
To those back home, while trying to convey
Their hopes and fears about our forces' progress.
Withholding news frustrates them in their role.
These opposed outlooks, not surprisingly,
At times cause bitter clashes and distrust.
Announcements of successful operations
Raise morale both at home and in the war zone.
But news of serious setbacks such as Fitzroy
Involving heavy casualties and losses
Straightaway prompts the unconvinced to ask:
Why do we fight this war and risk men's lives?

The wisdom of permitting 5-Brigade,
New to conditions met with in the Falklands
And ill-equipped with transport and supplies,
To undertake a fresh line of advance
Is called in question. Yet mishaps like Fitzroy
Have no one cause, but a grim combination —
Ill luck, ill judgement and mismanagement,
But overriding and compounding all,
Serious breakdowns in communication.

    *   *   *   *   *   *

The Task Force is reliably informed
That Stanley has been strongly garrisoned
With thirty companies — eight thousand men —
Well dug in on Mounts Harriet and Longdon,
Two Sisters, Tumbledown and Sapper Hill,
All ringed with mines and batteries of guns.
Menendez thinks his line impregnable.

The British troops are under no illusion
That capturing Port Stanley will be easy.
Only the mettle of Argentina's troops,
An army largely of young untrained conscripts
Is doubtful; though they showed clearly at Goose Green,
They can fight bravely and tenaciously.

Events at Fitzroy give sufficient warning
That future moves must not be left to chance.
So, in preparing for a final onslaught
Our troops make endless recces and patrols
To gauge the enemy's strength and dispositions.

Reports of hostile forces on West Falkland
Are checked by SAS. Near to Port Howard
Captain John Hamilton with his patrol
Disturbs the enemy force. Shot in the back,
He keeps returning fire till he is killed.
His superb leadership and bravery
Earn Hamilton a posthumous M.C.

Back east, the Mountain Arctic Warfare Cardre,
Patrolling ahead of British-held positions
Tackles a troop of Argentine commandos,
Destroying their post and taking prisoners.
Elsewhere patrols move forward every night
Probing for enemy minefields and defences
Often in waterlogged country. In the dark,
Patrols know every step brings hidden dangers.
A young marine treads in an unmarked minefield
Losing his foot with fearful suffering.

Elsewhere the enemy's fires are seen, although
He makes no challenge to our patrols.
A group with Chris Fox from 45-Commando
Confronts an Argentine outpost. In a fight
Commandos account for several of the foe
Before withdrawing. Through such raid missions
Our troops gain knowledge of the likely strength
And whereabouts of enemy formations.

Where to attack? Brigadier Waters favours
Thrusts towards Harriet and Mount Tumbledown;
So bypassing Mount Longdon and Two Sisters,
Where resistance will fade once they're outflanked.
Thompson prefers attacking on the whole front
From Harriet to Longdon. His view prevails.

Moore orders 3-Commando Brigade to attack
Mount Longdon, Two Sisters and Mount Harriet.
Next night Scots Guards, Welsh Guards and Gurkha Rifles
Pass through to storm Mounts Tumbledown and William.
3-Commando Brigade then resumes its attack,
The daily leap-frog giving the foe no rest
Until he cries 'Enough!'

Loss of *Atlantic Conveyor's* giant helicopters
Limits the British troop's mobility
In launching their combined assault on Stanley
Over steep, roadless, rugged countryside.

Sea Kings and Wessex fly unceasingly
Ferrying guns, supplies and ammunition,
Their pilots exhausted with fatigue and stress;
While maintenance crews, with unimagined skill
And sheer resource contrive to keep them flying.

Woodward advises Moore that new ship losses
Severely limit naval gun support
For the Army's onslaught upon Port Stanley.
Yet there is good news. Damaged *Argonaut*
Is cleared at last of unexploded bombs
By Brian Dutton's dedicated work
But still requires repair. While late next day
Avenger, targeted by an air-launched Exocet
Shoots down the missile with her 4.5-inch gun —
The final Exocet air-launched by the foe
In the Falklands War. Magnificient *Avenger!*

*   *   *   *   *   *   *

On hillsides held by British troops
Commanders brief their men
Detailing times, objectives, routes
With words exhorting them
To all-out effort. Major Vaux
Knows silence and surprise
Are vital for this final throw.
He makes men realise
Once started no one must relax:
42-Commandos' drive
Must go through minefields in attacks;
To fail will cost more lives.
The enemy is well dug-in
In well-defended posts
But once our main attack goes in
He'll soon give up the ghost.

All day men wait, watching the empty landscape.
They start to move at twilight, well aware
That the whole British force is moving forward.

Our guns bombard the enemy in earnest
From every point on land and from the sea.
Men freeze as enemy star-shells pierce the darkness
(Surely the slightest movement will betray us!)
Lighting up narrow pathways through the minefields.
42-Commando advances through open country.
One company gets lost; one fails to meet
The Welsh Guards on its flank; but Vaux ensures
All companies are in contact by the start time.

Backed up by heavy Naval and land-based gun-fire,
42-Commando scales Mount Harriet.
Nearing the top they meet with enemy fire.
K-Company rakes Argentine positions
With rockets and machine-guns, clearing bunkers
With small arms and grenades. But hostile gunfire
Wounds four marines. Then as he storms a gunpost,
Corporal Watts is wounded at close range.
He grabs the rifle but is then shot dead.
Corporal Newland, shot in both legs, remains,
Guiding his Section's attack by radio.
With countless daring and courageous deeds
K-Company secures Mount Harriet,
Capturing seventy enemy prisoners
With only one man killed — a prodigious feat!

Traversing difficult ground in growing darkness
45-Commandos reach their start line late.
Two Sisters' twin humps dimly loom before them.
X-Company takes the nearest peak in style
But then meets mortar and machine-gun fire.
66-calibre rockets clear the way
To let the advance resume. Z-Company
Storms a strongpoint unscathed. Unhappily
Y-Company loses two troop commanders
Injured by mortar fire. An engineer
Is killed while clearing mines. In heavy fire,
45-Commandos push home their attack
Slowly subduing enemy resistance.

After two hours, Two Sisters is secured.
Argentine soldiers, often leaderless
Lie inert, waiting to be taken prisoner.
When daylight comes, our men cannot believe
Troops would abandon posts so strongly built.

When giving gun-fire backing to the Army
Our ships invite attack by enemy missiles.
Warship *Glamorgan,* lending support by night
Detects an approaching missile. Straightaway
Sea Cat is fired; chaff is discharged; the ship
Turns stern about and makes full speed away
In vain. An Exocet, fired from ashore
Strikes the ship's upper deck, hangar and galley.

The blast destroys a Wessex helicopter —
Six men in the hangar dying instantly.
Fire takes hold; six more die in the galley.
Men struggle for two hours to quench the fires.
Though sturdy *Glamorgan* lives to fight again,
Many are burned and wounded, thirteen killed —
Among them gifted Lieutenant David Tinker
Who might himself have chronicled in full,
Had he been spared, the chequered Falklands story
Delineated in his verse and letters.

3-Parachute's advance towards Mount Longdon
Is soon in trouble. In B-Company
A corporal sets off a mine, the blast
Smashing his leg and drawing enemy fire.
Snipers of Seventh Argentine Regiment
Employing newest night-vision equipment
Pin down A-Company with deadly fire.

B-Company's assault upon the summit
Meets concentrated enemy resistance
By mortars, rifle-fire and machine-guns.
Paras inch up the hillside, using rockets
To blast the enemy. Platoon Commander
Lieutenant Bickerdyke receives a head wound.

Corporal Bailey, storming the bunker ahead
Meets the same fate. Platoon Sergeant McKay
Quickly regroups his men and charges forward,
Lobbing grenades into the enemy bunker
As he is killed. For conspicuous bravery
McKay is awarded a posthumous V.C.

Milan Groups support B-Company's advance
But are exposed to murderous enemy fire.
A direct hit from a recoil-less rifle
Wipes a Milan Team out. The deadly aim
Of enemy snipers hampers our advance.
Gough and Gray with grenades and bayonets
Charge a machine-gun post and take a captive.

B-Company regroups to try once more
To root out snipers firing from front and rear.
Its losses are severe: in 4-Platoon
Of twenty five men, twelve are left; in total
B-Company loses forty killed and wounded.
Hew Pike orders the Company to halt,
To let A-Company to pass through their positions,
And calls for more artillery support.

Stretcher bearers labour throughout the action
To carry casualties from the hillsides.
Medical teams work wonders with the wounded,
Many requiring treatment without delay;
In dire conditions, often in the open,
Doctors use all their skills and dedication
To succour the wounded and to save men's lives.

As dawn breaks, enemy fire begins to fade.
A-Company proceeds with bombs and rifles
To clear remaining enemy resistance.
In this, the bloodiest action in the Falklands
3-Para loses twenty-three men killed
And forty-seven men wounded, in one battle.

[End of Canto-IX]

61

CANTO X

TUMBLEDOWN : WIRELESS RIDGE : FOES SURRENDER!

The clearing mist reveals the vales below
Where fleeing foes are swiftly rounded up
To be sent back in groups as prisoners.
Daylight hampers 3-Brigade's next objective:
'To exploit ahead as far as Tumbledown',
The mountain stronghold commanding open ground
Devoid of cover for advancing troops.
Its men are ordered to consolidate
As 5-Brigade takes over the attack.

Men of Scots Guards, with Blues and Royal tanks
Are first in action, led by Major Bethell.
A mine blows up a Scorpion, but the crew
Escapes unhurt. The party reconnoitres
An enemy strong-post, seemingly abandoned.
At point blank range the enemy opens fire.
Caught in an ambush, Guardsmen fight their way
With small arms and grenades through enemy trenches.
Two Scots Guardsmen are killed; four more are wounded.
An injured Argentine throws a grenade,
Wounding two Britons, as he is shot dead.
Four more Guardsmen are wounded, two men lose feet
Stepping on mines while carrying wounded men.
Thus does the deadly minefield take its toll.

The main Scots Guards' attack is launched at nine.
Marching through snow showers, G-Company
Reaches its target without opposition.
Then as the Left Flank Company moves up
It meets fierce enemy machine-gun fire.
In a few moments snipers kill three Guardsmen.

Rocket-fire fails to weaken the defence
Of Argentina's crack force, the 5th Marines
Backed up by mortars and machine-gun fire.
Fierce fire persists till Major Kiszeley
Using grenades and with fixed bayonets
Spearheads a charge on enemy positions
With 15-Platoon. Kiszeley himself kills three.
After a bitter struggle up the hillside
Scots Guardsmen reach the crest of Tumbledown.
Immediately 15-Platoon Commander
And two more men are wounded. Only four
Are left to hold the hill till reinforced.
To gain its targets, Left Flank Company
Loses seven Guardsmen killed and twenty wounded.

In the last phase the Right Flank Company
Meets intense fire from snipers and machine-guns,
Losing a troop commander and three men.
With phosphorus grenades and automatics,
Guardsmen dislodge the enemy from his bunkers
Doggedly inching forward over rocks.
Capturing prisoners, they attack the foe
With bayonet and rifle. Fresh from England,
Lieutenant Robert Lawrence leads his men
Forward to silence a machine-gun post.

In the attack Lawrence is hit behind,
A high-velocity bullet piercing his brain,
Leaving him for dead — his head shot through.
Yet against all odds he lives. After six hours
Of murderous fire and violent opposition,
Guards seize Mount Tumbledown, though at the cost
Of nine men killed and forty-three men wounded.
A fearful toll in valiant lives ensures
The gateway to Port Stanley is secured.

As Guards seize Tumbledown, 2-Para's goal
Is to take Wireless Ridge, key starting point
For 3-Para's next phase of the assault.

A 'side show' to distract the enemy
Is planned by SAS. In four small boats
Backed by fierce fire from SAS patrols
They strafe the eastern end of Wireless Ridge.
The enemy replies with A.A. cannon,
Damaging all four craft. The planned diversion
Partly succeeds, but, seriously outgunned,
The raiding force withdraws with three men wounded.

Meanwhile 2-Para, bound for Wireless Ridge,
Endures a final lightning raid by Skyhawks
Yet moves away on time towards its targets —
Posts held by Argentina's 7th Regiment.
A lethal concentration of firepower —
Gun batteries, machine-guns, naval gun-fire,
Scorpions and Scimitars with cannon fire —
Assails the enemy while the Paras advance.
Within twelve hours, six thousand rounds are fired
With small response. Finally our bombardment
Has silenced the foe's machine-guns.
                                    D-Company
Gains its initial goal with small resistance.
Then, grimly skirting a reported minefield,
A and B Companies both arrive intact.
Lastly D-Company sweeps further eastward
To seize the forward slope of Wireless Ridge.
David Chaundler, 2-Para's new Commander
Flown out from Britain, learns with some relief
That Guards have taken hilltops facing the Ridge.

At rest, the Paras start to brew their tea
When word spreads that enemy is fleeing.
Along the whole front, Argentines are seen
In flight across the hills towards Port Stanley.
Young conscripts, keeping watch in foxholes for weeks,
Untrained, undisciplined and poorly led,
Knowing little about their country's war aims,
Often hungry and forced to search for food,
Finally unnerved by continual shelling,
Begin a general movement back to Stanley.

Is this a real retreat? Near Moody Brook
Sporadic enemy firing still continues.
2-Para's D-Company sees men emerge
From foxholes to join in the general flight.
For a few moments enemy paratroopers
Advance towards them. The Company's supply
Of live round almost gone, it now stands firm
Prepared to use fixed bayonets and grenades.
When heavy gun support is brought to bear,
The counter-attack dissolves. The group breaks up
And joins retreating Argentines heading east.

Chaundler reports this startling news to Thompson
Who sanctions an immediate advance.
At 2-Para's 'O' Group, Colonel Chaundler directs
B-Company to seize adjoining hilltops —
Blues and Royals' tanks to provide a firebase,
While A-Company makes speed towards Port Stanley.

Despite the news, troops still proceed with caution.
Sporadic shelling meets Welsh Guards and Gurkhas
Advancing towards Mount William and Sapper Hill.
With small resistance they secure these heights
That might have cost the British forces dear.
3-Para's battle plans for Moody Brook
Are halted by news that Farrar-Hockley's men
Have cleared the barracks and have now passed through.

Few signs of life are seen around Port Stanley.
A ship in harbour carries a white flag.
Then, in red berrets, led by Colonel Chaundler,
2-Para proudly marches into Stanley
On to the racecourse, where a paratrooper
Tears down the Argentine flag, and to wild cheering,
Once more raises aloft the Union Jack!

Moves for a ceasefire, already begun
By Rod Bell and Mike Rose, are now stepped up.

Appeals to move civilians from Port Stanley
Have been ignored; and sadly, in the night
Naval shelling has killed three Falkland ladies
Sleeping in their own home.
Dr. Alison Bleaney, in sole charge
Of Stanley Hospital, horrified by this news,
Phones an Argentine officer, Captain Hussey,
Imploring him to act on these appeals.

British ship *Fearless* signals the Argentines:
'The position of your forces is now hopeless.
British forces suround you.' The message warns them
They should surrender to save further bloodshed.

Hussey consults with General Menendez
Who sanctions talks. Rod Bell and Rose fly in
By helicopter. They persuade the General
To end hostilities, and to surrender
His force in East Falkland; also (under duress)
The remnant in West Falkland. Argentine troops
Will be transported home in British ships.

General Moore arrives. Terms are agreed.
Both generals sign the document drawn up,
So ending the Falklands War, with the surrender
Of all the Argentine forces on the Islands —
Crowning the epic struggle of our Task Force
　　　　　with Falklands Victory!

[End of Canto-X]

FALKLANDS VICTORY:

EPILOGUE

CONCLUSION

The shooting ends; and now begins the task
Of grappling with the legacies of war.
The dead are buried; the greatest care is taken
Of many badly wounded. (Unhappily
New weapons intensify the injuries they inflict!)
Wounded men fly to Fitzroy or Teal Inlet;
More serious cases straight to Ajax Bay
Or to Uganda, *now free to be berthed*
In Stanley Harbour. Critically wounded men
Are flown to England for intensive treatment.

The Task Force offers thanks and pays its tributes
To the war's victims. In Stanley's cathedral
A Service of Thanksgiving is conducted
By Padre David Cooper. There next day,
Three ladies killed by British shells on Stanley
Are laid to rest. Falklanders cast no blame
On British troops, but give thanks for their freedom.

At Bluff Cove Welsh Guards sorrowfully gather
To take a final leave of fifty comrades
Killed on Sir Galahad. *The ship, still burning,*
Is towed away to be sunk as a war grave,
While choirs of Welsh Guards sing 'Land of My Fathers'.
Lastly, beneath a cross on Darwin Hill
Placed there by settlers from Darwin and Goose Green,
Remembering men who fell nearby in battle,
Paratroops meet to honour their dead comrades.

Eleven thousand Argentine prisoners
Are put on British ships and taken home.
For many, little older than mere schoolboys
Thrust into war by government decree,
The Falklands made a brief unhappy bridge
To sudden manhood. Many will retain
Grim memories of hardship and privation
Compulsorily borne for national pride.

Promptly, its mission ended, Britain's Task Force
Disperses, after witnessing the transfer
Of rule of the Islands back to Falklanders.
Commanders are recalled home to report
Upon the campaign's circumstance and outcome.
Fighting units, depleted, battle weary,
Gladly resign the Falkland Isles' defence
To fresh contingents; grateful for the chance
To rest, recoup and see their homes once more.

The Royal Navy can at last review
The damage done to its embattled warships
And programme their refit.
Its ships' crews, many of whom had been at sea
For several months, enjoy a well-earned shore leave.
The Royal Air Force likewise directs its squadrons
Homewards, content to relinquish its patrols
Of Falklands skies to squadrons just arriving.

Restoring power and water to Port Stanley
Is quickly put in hand. War-damaged houses
Are reconstructed; others are replaced
With prefabricated dwellings shipped from Europe.
A start is made on cleansing up the Islands —
Spent shells and bullets littering the camp,
Hiding grim heaps of bombs and live explosives —
Finding and marking recklessly-sown minefields
That form a hidden danger still today —
Removing spoils of war — The spoils of war!
None flow from modern war; war but despoils.

The moods of hope, of fear, of apprehension
As Britain's fortunes in the Falklands see-sawed
At home now turn to joy, with jubilation
That troops at last are free from combat dangers.
The nation celebrates their victory
In a Service of Thanksgiving in Saint Paul's.
A Victory Parade is held in London.
Large crowds at Portsmouth, Plymouth and Southampton
Greet the returning ships and welcome home
The members of the Task Force. **Canberra**
Is met by an armada of small boats,
By hosts of relatives and well-wishers.

Britain acknowledges its Falklands heroes.
Outstanding acts of courage and distinction
In combat, in support, in rescue work,
Are recognised. War-Correspondents too
Are honoured. Yet many more not named may claim:
'We too saw service in the Falklands Campaign'.

Conditions in the Falklands slowly quieten.
Sir Rex Hunt returns, now as Commissioner.
New engineering works are set in train —
An airfield, deepened harbours, metalled roads —
Developments designed to improve the Islands'
Economy and defences. Falklanders
Welcome the workers who arrive from Britain
Enlivening the scene with warmth and humour.

Yet some reflect, had Britain in time provided
Improvements requested, she would now be spared
Many more millions. Timely expense by London
Would have warned Argentines to hesitate
Before they ventured to invade the Falklands.

Appraisal of the Task Force operation
Decides where innovations are required:
Warship defences against fire and missiles
Need reinforcement. The performance design
Of aircraft, weapons, instruments and transport
Calls for fresh study. The soldier's marching boot,
Unsuited to this terrain, receives — the boot!

The dovetailing of joint-service commands,
Vital when mounting combined operations
Gets top-level study. Failures in the Falklands
Are largely ascribed to poor communications
Preventing complete liaison between staffs.

Returning servicemen fit uneasily
Into a post-war world. Many continue
Noteworthy careers in their country's forces;
Others seek roles in civil occupations.
The transition bears hardest on the wounded.
Burn victims undergo repeated treatment
In painful and demeaning circumstances
While specialists reshape disfigurements.
Many require to make painful adjustments
To come to terms with disability.
Rob Lawrence, shockingly wounded in Tumbledown,
Though left for dead, miraculously survives,
Showing man's power to both maim and heal.
He lives, a proof of man's tenacity,
Despite all suffering and obloquy.

Falklanders feel safe once more. In Argentina,
Galtieri resigns: The Junta falls.
Anaya and Lami Dozo lose their posts.
All three are tried and jailed for negligence
In prosecuting the Malvinas War.
New President Alfonsin promises
No further invasion, but declines to make
Formal announcement that the war is ended —
Until Britain has agreed to undertake
Negotiations over sovereignty.
Britain refuses to negotiate
Until Argentina ends hostilities...
(Little has changed!)
So Falklanders' relations with their neighbours
Stay distant; though more recent overtures
By Argentina's next President, Carlos Menem,
Give hope the impasse may one day be broken.

In Britain the cause and conduct of the conflict
Bring serious criticism of the Government.
Yet the Franks Committee largely supports their action,
Exonerating Ministers from blame.
The Cabinet grants Falkland Islanders
Full British Citizenship, while pushing forward
Developments already placed in hand.

Slowly, the Falklands' economy improves.
The new Mount Pleasant Airport at Port Stanley
Handles long-distance jet planes flown from Britain,
Thus opening up the route for businessmen,
And speedy journeys back home for Islanders.
Hotels and shops add colour to Stanley's High Street.
Large hauls of fish lure fishing fleets to the Falklands,
Where Fishing Permits yield large revenues.
The Islands' site as gateway to the Antarctic
Elevate their importance: bidding fair
To heighten rival claims to sovereignty.

Aggression halted; status quo restored;
Conventional justice is therefore satisfied.
Unchecked aggression kindles further aggression:
Vide Hitler, vide examples — numberless —
In recent times. Today's society
Has means to halt but not prevent aggressors.
Nations must therefore maintain vigilance
Or they will strike again. Was Galtieri
Merely an opportunist? Violence
Too often strikes when men are off their guard!
As perfidy, Galtieri's crimes were slight;
Viewed against history's cavalcade of carnage
The Falklands War was small. Yet one may ask:
Had Argentina any moral right
To take up arms 'to gain a patch of ground'
She claimed as hers? Did not duplicity
Debase Britain's endless prevarication
In talks on sovereignty? To justify
Their actions, men rely on principles.

Britons cite precedence and established rule:
Argentines, their former dominion usurped —
Tenets supported by historical precepts.
But does the outcome justify **Belgrano,**
Sheffield *or Fitzroy? Land despoiled by mines?...*
Violence must be stopped; yet one may ask
Why, even now, brave officers and men
Still pay the price with lives and injuries
To get unheeding governments off the hook.

What of the future? Can two thousand souls
Command, for ever, assured defence and aid
From half a world away? In days to come,
On this point, Britons may have much to say.
Whate'er befalls, Britain should leave no doubt
Over her future policies and objectives,
But safeguard them with adequate resources.
Twice in this century, uncertainty
About her intentions has given rise to war.

May the time come
When men no longer settle their disputes
By threat or force; when common sense and reason
Rather than self-concern solve differences;
When kelpers' lives again are undisturbed
By world affairs; when seals and albatross
Lie unmolested on the wind-swept shores
Of the once-more tranquil Falklands, as they ride
The South Atlantic tide.

[The End]